Bestselling author Michele Slung, herself an
only child, has collected the reminiscences of
famous only children. These writers,
actors, politicians, and other prominent
persons speak their piece on the subject of
their only-ness and what it has meant to
their lives. From Hans Christian Andersen
to Indira Gandhi to Frank Sinatra, an
uncommon variety of only children go on
record in this delightful collection of anecdotes,
observations, and personal reflections that
strike close to home and right to the heart.

THE ONLY CHILD BOOK

Also by Michele Slung:

CRIME ON HER MIND: *Fifteen
Stories of Female Sleuths from the
Victorian Era to the Forties*

MOMILIES*

THE ABSENT-MINDED
PROFESSOR'S MEMORY BOOK*

MORE MOMILIES*

*Published by Ballantine Books

THE
ONLY CHILD
BOOK

❧

Michele Slung

BALLANTINE BOOKS • NEW YORK

CREDITS

This book is dedicated to my fellow only children: We are *not* alone.

Being an only child is a disease in itself.

G. Stanley Hall,
"THE CONTENTS OF CHILDREN'S MINDS" (1883).

FOREWORD

I've always taken it for granted that I'm an only child, and it's always seemed, frankly, like a good thing. No need to share my toys or books or my parents' attention, and no problems, whatsoever, in the creation of a sturdy little ego that has, ever since, stood me in good stead.

I don't say I wasn't curious about the loud and frequently untidy households I hung out at, containing families larger than three. But, looking back at it now, I think I was actually rather bored by my friends' siblings and probably wondered why they weren't, as well. (The point is, of course, you can choose your friends, but when it comes to your relations you have no choice.)

Since I grew up in the fifties, the epithet "spoiled brat," then so freely tossed around, seems to have grown up with me, and I really don't hear it uttered very often anymore.* But the clichés and confusion about only childhoods

---

*Except in reference to China, where "spoiled brats," or "little emperors," as they're known there, are actually a major social problem today, owing to that nation's controversial family-planning program. The result of the stringent, even brutal, attempts to limit couples to one baby means that, according to projections, by the year 2000, the majority of Chinese twenty-year-olds will be from single-child families. Notes Lena H. Sun of

persist, and a look at the past thirty years' worth of articles in newspapers and magazines reveals nothing new.

"Only—Not Lonely!" "Only Children: The Family of the Future." "Do Only Kids Have More Fun?" These same titles recur over and over again. In the meantime, earnest psychologists write books, hoping to dispel persistent notions that we onlies are inescapably neurotic, if not mad, bad, and dangerous to the social fabric.

Recently what they seem to be saying, having reduced us to statistics, is that in such readily measurable things as intelligence, health, education, and salary—as well as in the more subjective areas of self-confidence and emotional stability—the similarities between onlies and others are actually more important than the differences.

All well and good, of course, and useful for reassuring those increasing numbers of single-child parents (according to the Census Bureau, a

The Washington Post, 'Fat brats' are also on the rise, since not only do the Chinese prefer chubby children to thin ones, but, with only-child households, all the sugary treats and extra suppertime morsels find their way into one little mouth."

"...Single-child parents are not just feeding and clothing their children and escorting them to and from kindergarten, they are making history," writes one Chinese magazine.

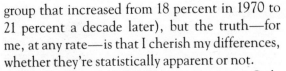

group that increased from 18 percent in 1970 to 21 percent a decade later), but the truth—for me, at any rate—is that I cherish my differences, whether they're statistically apparent or not.

Thus, when I decided to investigate Only Child-dom—the world of only children—I quickly realized that the academic route of facts, figures, and theories was not the one I wanted to take. Granted, it was fascinating to learn that no U.S. president so far has been sibling-less (it's not fair, by my lights, to count FDR, since he had an older half brother), that only children are more likely to have collecting hobbies and are "superior in nearly all forms of verbal activity."

And it was refreshing to come across the pair of only-child specialists who admitted that, though they'd devoted their careers to studying the phenomenon, when they played "Spot the Only" with new acquaintances, their success was "largely a matter of luck."

Then, there was the woman I met who told me that she, her husband, and their daughter were all only children. The punch line to the story: One night, when each of them was in a separate room of their apartment, quietly reading, the phone rang. In answer to the friend's query, "What are you all doing?" she heard herself reply, "Sitting at home, spending the evening

together." Or, at least, she said, chuckling at the memory, that's how three only children might define "together."

I discovered that a small group of Chicagoans had started Only Child International, and so I contacted James F. Henry, one of the founders. He informed me, with regret, that OCI had never really gotten off the ground, but mailed me a copy of the sole newsletter they managed to print. "It, like its parents," he noted wryly in the covering letter, "has no siblings."

And, reading that Sarah, Duchess of York, had gone on record saying she and Prince Andrew planned to have only one child, I hoped she'd stick to her guns and not be influenced by such published dicta as "the parents of an only child have no margin of error."

But, these odd bits and pieces aside, what I really wanted to do was squarely in the mold of predictable only-child behavior—I wanted an excuse to go to the library and encounter my fellow onlies within the pages of books. It's there, after all, that one can meet both the quick and the dead (and I even, occasionally, couldn't resist straying over toward the fictional).

What familiar actors, writers, statesmen, musicians, sports figures, scientists, and artists had been, like me, the sole apple of the parental eye? How had they reacted? What had been their circumstances? What had been the lasting effects? What memories had risen to the surface, and were these various individual recollections greatly distinct, one from the other? Did patterns form? Could it be said that most only children feel one way about their being "only," whether that one way be happy or sad, content or bitter?

Well, I'm going to let you, the readers of *The Only Child Book,* judge for yourself. And I'd also like to see if what happened to me, as I began to listen to these voices, will happen to you. That is to say, hearing the thoughts, feelings, and anecdotes of myriad childhoods triggered in me a sort of self-analysis. And all these only children— from Beryl Markham to Margaret Truman, from Jean-Paul Sartre to Frank Sinatra—began to seem as though they lined the sides of a corridor I was running down, nodding to me, waving, perhaps even cheering me on.

Not only that, but I also started to picture these folk conversing with one another—a *true* Only Child International—in just the way that so many of them had once spent hours talking to imaginary playmates.

What's more, I don't think that any insights

gained from the voices here will be limited just to only children or those directly involved with them (parents, spouses, lovers, friends, teachers, coworkers, etc.). Rather, since we know that childhood itself is a condition we all have in common, I believe that these often poignant and deeply felt emotional vignettes will unlock something in everyone, reminding us how those long-ago years are still alive inside of us, each and every day, until our memories shut down.

To be human is to be special; to be an only child is simply another kind of specialness, one that I urge you to appreciate.

ACKNOWLEDGMENTS

The following people went out of their way to help me during various stages of the research for this project. I wish to express my gratitude for their generosity and enthusiasm: Biography Bookshop (Carolyn Epstein, Chuck Mullen, Ted Woods), Nell Blaine, Antonia Boyle, Joan Brandt, Elisabeth Bumiller, R.L. Clarke, James F. Henry, Rick Hertzberg, Frank Mankiewicz, Nigel Nicolson, Deedy Ogden, Magnus Ringborg, Ednamae Storti, William Weaver.

And I'd like also to acknowledge, with affection, some only children who have been my friends: Kathy, Judy, Sappho, Gail, Chris, Ken, Claudine and Jean Ray, Shahnaz, Julio, Rebecca, and Alex.

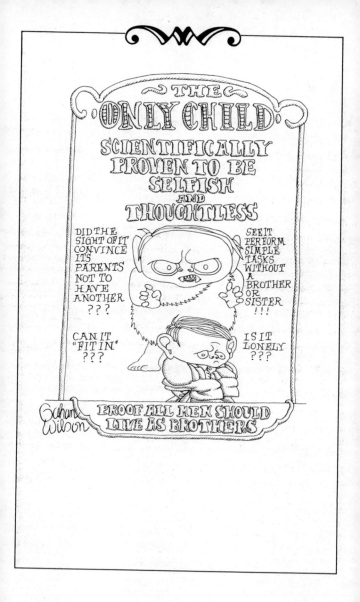

THE
ONLY CHILD
BOOK

This only child will always be remembered as
Scarlett O'Hara.

I am not saying that mothers should be prevented from loving their young. I am only saying that they should have someone else to love as well. If my mother had had a husband or a lover I would not have spent my days dying of thirst beside so many fountains.

Romain Gary,
WRITER

Dad, like all fathers, naturally only said good things. Many of his letters proudly discussed different aspects of my debut and career. As his only "baby," he would have probably backed me whatever I did after I got my college degree. But deep down, like many fathers of a career woman, especially when she's an only child, there was one thing that Dad wanted even more than to see me be a singer. He wanted to be a grandfather.

Margaret Truman,
WRITER AND DAUGHTER OF
PRESIDENT HARRY S. TRUMAN

Secrecy was my passion. I daresay that was why I hated companions. . . . I wasn't unhappy, only

solitary, but I don't pretend that I minded solitude, I rather chose it.

Vita Sackville-West,
WRITER

I feel sure that unborn babies pick their parents. They may spend a whole lifetime trying to figure out the reasons for their choice, but nothing in any human story is accidental.

Because I was so shy, I didn't make friends easily. I had no brothers or sisters, so I slowly had to get used to being alone; and like every only child, I seemed to spend more time with my parents than most children did. Even in my prayers at night, there were just the three of us. I used to kneel and say my prayers out loud. They were the same every night. "Now I lay me down to sleep. I pray the Lord my soul to keep. If I should die before I wake I pray the Lord my soul to take. God bless Daddy and God bless Mommy and make me a good girl." After I climbed into bed I always added a silent prayer that God would somehow find a way for me to get out of going to school without being sick.

Gloria Swanson,
ACTRESS

This only child was a poet best known for
his *Cantos*.

What the child psychologists would call the group spirit was found to be quite lacking in my personality.... I suppose it was only natural that the fact that I was unable to come to terms with my associates forced me to take refuge ever more intently within the shelter of my own imagination. I clearly recall that in my first months of school the periods of the day I most abhorred were not those devoted to work but, rather, those devoted to organized relaxation.

Glenn Gould,
PIANIST

Scorning any satisfaction to be derived from juvenile teamwork, Gould wouldn't even cooperate when it came to singing "Three Blind Mice" and entering the round at the correct moment. This recalcitrance enraged his teacher who eventually broke a piece of chalk over his head. "It is a truly ironic gesture," he told an interviewer, "that the subject in which I first won unfavorable distinction was, indeed, music."

Gorbachev's official biography is little more than a bare-bones list of Communist Party offices

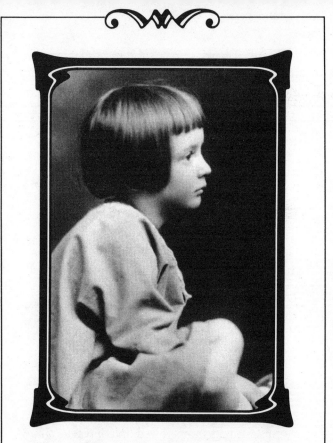

This only child, a poet and novelist, wrote of her
early life in *I Knew a Phoenix.*

held, and it lacks some of the most elementary information. For example, it is not known for certain whether he has any siblings. Some Soviets say he has a brother who works in agriculture, but no one seems to know the man's name or age. Reports of a sister cannot be confirmed.

Time, January 4, 1988

Even Kremlinologists are aware of the importance of only childhoods.

❦

"I hope you'll consider having another baby. It was lonely for me. Very lonely."

Frank Sinatra,
ENTERTAINER

Sinatra made this remark to his daughter Nancy, after the birth of her first child. However, Bob Anthony, one of his boyhood friends, had this to say of Sinatra's early years: "Being an only child made all the difference.... Frank had more. He didn't have to share with brothers and sisters. He even had his own bedroom. None of the rest of us had

This only child ruled the Soviet Union
from 1941-53.

half of what he had. He wore brand-new black-and-whites that his mother bought him, while the rest of us wore old oxfords that were hand-me-downs. He even had his own charge account at Geismer's department store. He had so many pairs of fancy pants from that store that we called him 'Slacksy O'Brien.' No question about it. Frank was the richest kid on the block."

I had fantasy friends I talked to. My parents and I were very close. We traveled a lot.

Divine,
ACTOR

Home has always been for me an idea as difficult as it is beguiling. Part of this feeling, I have no doubt, comes from the biographical fact that I don't so much come from a nuclear family as from a sub-atomic one. As a result, I remain irrationally jealous of anyone who boasts a large, close-knit family; irrationally jealous and immediately fascinated. I have spent most of my life

trying to find just such a family to graft myself onto—like a barnacle looking for a battleship.

David Rieff,

WRITER-EDITOR AND SON OF SUSAN SONTAG

I do not know
One of my sex; no woman's face remember,
Save from my glass, mine own; nor have I seen
More that I may call men than you, good friend,
And my dear father. How features are abroad,
I am skilless of; but, by my modesty,
The jewel in my dower, I would not wish
Any companion in the world but you,
Nor can imagination form a shape,
Besides yourself, to like of.

Miranda,
The Tempest, Act III, scene i

Until the magical shipwreck, depositing Fer-
dinand and his companions on the island,
Miranda's world has been peopled only by her
father, Prospero, his half-human servant, Cali-
ban, and the invisible sprite, Ariel.

This only child wrote *The Little Foxes* and had an enduring relationship with Dashiell Hammett.

Within our house, too, there was little change. My grandparents did not die, though they seemed very old. My father continued to teach at the high school; he had secured the job shortly after I was born. No one else was born. I was an only child. A great many only children were born in 1932. I make no apologies. I do not remember ever feeling the space for a competitor within the house.

John Updike,
WRITER

I was born an only child in Vienna. I must have been some eight or nine years old, because Hitler came when I was ten, and this was before Hitler came.

My mother had taken me to a *jause*—a tea party. I do remember a lot of little cakes and a lot of ladies and the boredom of their conversation. I don't remember that afterward, as my mother was buttoning my coat in the foyer. I was heard to say, "Here no one knows anything, here no one talks about anything."

In the surprised silence my mother asked me what I meant.

I said, "Here nobody knows that I am learning

13

to dance on my toes. Here nobody talks about my figure skating."

My mother says that she determined then and there never again to talk about me to other people—at least not in my hearing, a resolution she did not keep because I only know this story from having heard her tell it.

Lore Segal,
WRITER

I have 54 first cousins. A number of them became ersatz siblings, so I have never *felt* like an only child.

Christopher Buckley,
WRITER AND SON OF WILLIAM F. BUCKLEY, JR.

But after dinner, alas, I was soon obliged to leave Mamma, who stayed talking with the others, in the garden if it was fine, or in the little parlour where everyone took shelter when it was wet. Everyone except my grandmother, who held that "It's a pity to shut oneself indoors in the country," and used to have endless arguments with my father on the very wettest days, because he

This only child crooned bobby-soxers
into frenzies.

would send me up to my room with a book instead of letting me stay out of doors. "That is not the way to make him strong and active," she would say sadly, "especially this little man, who needs all the strength and will-power he can get."

Narrator,
REMEMBRANCE OF THINGS PAST

Proust's biographer tells us that, although Marcel had a brother, Robert, to whom he was devoted, "in [the autobiographical] A la Recherche, although no doubt his reasons were mainly aesthetic, he preferred to abolish Robert entirely." In art, if not in life, he could have his adored mother to himself.

I actually have the French government to thank for my present-day physique. Back then, my father, as head cook, would always save the best cut of steak for me, his only child.

Jackie Chan,
KUNG FU STAR

As a baby, Chan Kwong Sang (Chan's real name) nearly was sold for a paltry sum when his parents, poor Hong Kong immigrants, couldn't afford to feed him. The family situa-

This only child is the daughter of the 33rd
President of the United States and now writes
mystery novels.

*tion improved, however, after both his mother
and father took jobs as servants at the French
consulate there.*

❧

To say I was in love again will vex the reader
beyond endurance, but he must remember that
being in love had a peculiar meaning for me. I
had never even been kissed and love was an ideal
based on the exhibitionism of the only-child. It
meant a desire to lay my personality at someone's
feet as a puppy deposits a slobbery ball; it meant a
non-stop daydream, a planning of surprises, an
exchange of confidences, a giving of presents, an
agony of expectation, a delirium of impatience,
ending with the premonition of boredom more
drastic than the loneliness which it set out to
cure.

Cyril Connolly,
WRITER AND CRITIC

❧

Before going to school, I don't remember playing
with any children. Playing with children of my
age was synonymous with what we as adults
rather awkwardly try to say when we use an

expression like "having a relationship" with children of my age. As an only child with parents who did not happen to know or find congenial any other parents whatever with children of my own age, I don't remember ever playing with a child at home, in anyone else's home, in a "swingie" (a playground with swings, roundabouts, seesaws, etc.) or anywhere.

R. D. Laing,
PSYCHIATRIST

As the only child of a banker-hunter and fisherman father and a Southern belle-type mother, I grew up feeling all things were possible. My father talked to me of The Russian Five-Year Plan when I was six and expected me to understand. He took me hunting and fishing with him while my mother took me to the theater, taught me to dance and make myself up "pretty." I had total security and love. As a small child I invented a make-believe sister whose name was Mary. She was a delightful companion because she did everything with me, but always a little less successfully. She played games with me, but I always won. I enjoyed some solitude and since adulthood have continued to feel the need to get

This only child wrote many books, including
The Edwardians and *Pepita,* but she is, perhaps,
best remembered for her friendship with
Virginia Woolf.

away occasionally from the madding crowd to recharge my batteries and get my balance. Although I missed the companionship of siblings in my youth, I feel that I benefitted from that total love, attention and security my parents gave me.

Katherine Fanning,
FORMER EDITOR,
THE CHRISTIAN SCIENCE MONITOR

∽

I was an only child, and then, when I was 7, my parents split up, and I was even more alone. I wasn't very good at schoolwork, but what I did learn was to entertain myself.

Jonathan Winters,
COMEDIAN

∽

Loneliness, however, the birthright of the only child, held no particular terrors for me.... Being alone was easier, I discovered, if you became two people, the actor and the observer. The observer was always the same, the actor played many parts: an officer in the Foreign Legion, for instance, or a ruthless private detective with rooms in Half Moon Street, or a Brigadier in

Napoleon's army. "There he goes," I was able to say about myself, even in the deeply unhappy days when I lolloped about a frozen football field, keeping as far as possible from the ball, "cantering across the burning sands with his crack platoon of Spahis (ex-murderers, robbers and at least one Duke disappointed in love, but whoever asked questions of a Legionnaire?) in search of the tents of Mahmoud Bey, and a levelling of the score after the disgrace of Sidi Benoud."

Later my character became more sophisti-cated, as I came more under the influence of Noël Coward and Dornford Yates.

John Mortimer,
WRITER

As childhood progresses, a time is reached when there is very rapid acceleration of change in the character of fantasy; this change is in the direc-tion of burying, losing interest in, forgetting, or modifying what may in very early childhood have been truly incredible fantastic imaginary playmates, and toward a direction of attempting to personify playmates very like oneself.... But even in the case of children who have grown up

This only child gave the world such musicals as
Kiss Me, Kate.

with no possibility of playing with other children, who are born on remote farms, or in other isolated places, this change in play or change in imagination appears. The child now appears to have rather realistic imaginary playmates, while before a great deal of his imaginary accouterments, his imaginary toys, were strikingly fantastic.

Harry Stack Sullivan,
PSYCHIATRIST

Sullivan was himself an only child.

I was an only child and overprotected. I never had a cat because a little neighbor had her eye put out by hers. I never was allowed a pair of roller skates because one of my mother's cousins fractured his skull on the edge of a sidewalk in Arles in 1911. But I had canaries and goldfish. When they died the fact would be hidden from me, and they would be replaced the same night by live ones, which were not always the same size or color.

Simone Signoret,
ACTRESS

I was not an adventurous boy, except in thought.

A. J. Ayer,
PHILOSOPHER

I had the priceless advantage of being an only child. All the love that I might have had to share with rival siblings was mine alone. The nest was mine, so that the affection and interest of these totally dissimilar people was concentrated on me. "I never wanted another child," said Mother, "I stopped at perfection" (not a bad thing to have said about one). For sixteen glorious years I was totally secure. Love was everywhere, and I knew that I was the living link between Father and Mother. Sixteen years of that kind of security helps one withstand almost any blow that life can deal. One is firmly rooted like the bamboo, one bends, but does not break.

Brooke Astor,
PHILANTHROPIST

If there had been someone to show me animals or flowers, or taught me how to be happily alone with a book, what love, what blessing I would

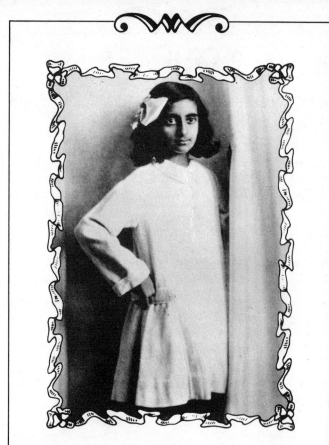

This only child became the prime minister of
India, like her father before her.

have had in my heart for him. Instead of which, I walked myself to standstill...and *passed* the time ...which I would later never find long enough. Theseus came into the world in an underground chamber, no matter, he came up like a shoot from a plant: but I grew up in absolute nothingness, up towards nothing.

Rainer Maria Rilke,
POET

My first memories go back to the time when I lived with my mother in a little apartment. I was the only child and we two were alone in the world; my father died when I was two.

Anna Pavlova,
BALLERINA

Very little air found its way into the hotel; the ferns in their brass tubs gave out a fetid smell like dying jungle vegetation. Now and then someone took me for a boring walk in Kensington Gardens, and once I was treated to a visit to the Natural History Museum, but for the most part I was left to my own devices—filling a bath to float a little, lopsided sailing-boat; drawing fierce battle

This only child is best remembered for his role in
The Thin Man.

scenes; teasing a tired old maid or building card-houses on the floor of the "Residents Lounge."

Alec Guinness,
ACTOR

This describes a school vacation taken at age six when young Alec was "confined to a rather gloomy London hotel in the Cromwell Road."

I was a silent boy who went by reading. My father did not use these words. I was, in retrospect, a very funny little boy. I was so alone I did not know how to swear, but, clamoring, they taught me. I wanted to belong, to enter the troglodytes' existence. I shouted and mouthed the uncouth, unfamiliar words with the rest.

Loren Eiseley,
NATURALIST

Eiseley's mother, his father's second wife, was completely deaf.

I was the only child of a divorced mother with her own business to run, and the

hours were long between the end of the school day and the time when my mother came home from her shop, I filled them with make-believe and reading. Whenever she could, my mother took me to the theater in San Francisco, and my yearnings focused upon that stage.

My desire for siblings had been demonstrated at the age of four, when I kidnapped a baby parked by its trusting mother outside the Mill Valley Post Office.

Eve Arden,
ACTRESS

The big legacy of only childness was, I think, a stupendous vocabulary at a young age. Spending most of my time with adults, which I suspect is the fate of only children, I had a knock-your-socks-off selection of words at my disposal as a kid. Permanently established in family lore is my use of the word "procrastinate." At age three, I would ask people why they were "procrastinating." I would also make reference to the "caduceus," the winged staff with two serpents twined around it. This was the symbol of the medical profession and, of course, a physician was a close friend of the family.

These words did not come from the "Dick and Jane" books, and—surprise!—I had a mother who was inordinately proud of my word power.

Margo Howard,

WRITER AND DAUGHTER OF ANN LANDERS

What it was going to be now, brothers, was homeways and a nice surprise for dadada and mum, their only son and heir back in the family bosom. Then I could lay back on the bed in my own malenky den and slooshy some lovely music, and at the same time I could think over what to do now with my jeezny.

Alex,
A Clockwork Orange

Author Anthony Burgess grew up as an only child.

Comparing Christmas gifts with other kids didn't take long or give much satisfaction, and even then the day was overshadowed by the harsh rule that I was not supposed to call at other children's houses or they mine. This, Mother said, was the family season, which was all very well for those who had families but death to an only child. It was the end of the season of imagination, and there was no reason to think it would ever come again. Nothing had happened as it happened in the Christmas number. There was no snow; no relative had returned from the States with presents for everyone; there was nothing but Christmas Mass and the choir thundering out *Natum videte regem angelorum*, as though they believed it, when any fool could see that things were going on in the same old way.

Frank O'Connor,
SHORT-STORY WRITER AND DIRECTOR OF THE
ABBEY THEATRE

Despite the title of O'Connor's thoroughly Irish memoir, An Only Child, *the book is more about family and place than it is about the state of siblingless-ness.*

∾

This way I have of talking, whether, as now, with my pencil, running on and on, or in my thoughts, is for me, another inheritance bequeathed to me long ago by my mother, who,

This only child turned into the most influential
political columnist of his time.

poor dear, saw heaven only knows what magic gifts in me....She was delighted when she saw how self-sufficient I was as a child, and how I used to talk to the chair, or to other objects close at hand, which for me, in their silence, contained a great enchantment—and they seemed to listen patiently to me, who demanded no answer.

Eleonora Duse,
ACTRESS

Duse appeared on stage as her mother's understudy beginning at the age of twelve.

I remember the very first time that I ever felt lonely. I was twenty-three and had just fallen in love. It took me a long time to recognize what the emotion was.

John Cleese,
ACTOR

I learned very soon when I was "in the way," and I found it pleasanter to be alone. When I was punished I was often shut in a dark closet to think over my faults, or to be frightened out of them. But I enjoyed the dark and the quiet, and I would soon be asleep.

...I saw very little of other children. My father did not approve of the neighbors; they were ignorant, common. I was made to understand that we were somehow better than the families that lived around us. But, periodically, early in the night, when I was supposed to be asleep, I overheard allusions to my "lonely childhood" and the repeated insistence that "it was not good for her." After every such discussion there would follow a period of visiting other farms to spend a day with Esther Summers, or Vida, or Jimmy Allen, or playing next door with the Brown boys. I did not especially enjoy those excursions; I was too used to being alone, to making my own games, and reveling in an unconscious enjoyment of the fields and trees and the birds.

Mary Astor,
ACTRESS

∞

Being an only child of poor working-class parents who, after they came home from the shop, were exhausted and harassed, I soon came to feel that loneliness was an inescapable fact of life—not

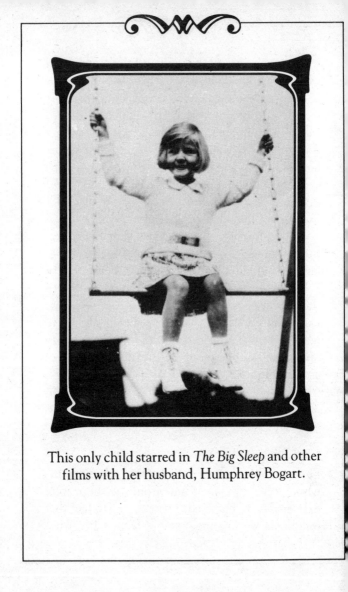

This only child starred in *The Big Sleep* and other films with her husband, Humphrey Bogart.

only of my life, but the life of everyone. When I saw the close and often happy ties between my own children, I felt a certain surprise and—let me admit it—jealousy. For by now loneliness has become ingrained, and while it can be relieved, it cannot be removed.

That is the main heritage of being an only child—the loneliness that scars, but also the loneliness that gives freedom to one's imagination.

Irving Howe,
WRITER AND EDITOR

∾

I was the only child and extremely spoiled, but I continually heard from my mother how very much happier I was than she had been, and that I was brought up like a nobleman's child.

Hans Christian Andersen,
FAIRY TALE WRITER

∾

My mother always claimed that I had taught myself to read, and very likely I did, since I can't remember a period when the printed word did not make its corresponding sound in my head as I

looked at it.... My grandmother Bowles visited us. I overheard her telling my mother, exactly as though I were'nt present, that precocity should not be encouraged; she foresaw disaster unless I were somehow brought into contact with other children, so that I could "grow in other directions." I did not know what she meant, but I immediately determined not to accept other direction.

Paul Bowles,
WRITER

Jane Bowles, his wife, also had no brothers and sisters. A childhood friend once described her as "very private, very early, as if there was a moat around her."

∾

I wish I'd had 10 brothers and 11 sisters.
Frederick Wiseman,
DOCUMENTARY FILMMAKER

∾

My mother's childbirth had been dangerously botched by a fashionable doctor in New Orleans, and forever after she stood in fear of going

This only child was the model for
Christopher Robin.

This only child, born in a vaudeville trunk, went from *Andy Hardy* to *Sugar Babies*.

through it again, and so I was an only child. (Twenty-one years later, when I was married and pregnant, she was frightened for me, and unashamedly happy when I lost the child.) I was thirty-four years old, after two successful plays, and fourteen or fifteen years of heavy drinking in a nature that wasn't comfortable with anarchy, when a doctor told me about the lifelong troubles of an only child. Most certainly I needed a doctor to reveal for me the violence and disorders of my life, but I had always known about the powers of an only child.

Lillian Hellman,
PLAYWRIGHT

I was left to myself a good deal. My father and my mother, Kamala, were often in jail. My father didn't believe in giving directions about what I should do or feel. I had to decide things regardless of his or anyone else's ideas. That was both good and bad, but it helped make me independent. I learned from my parents by example; they made me aware that a certain standard must be maintained, even when nothing was said.

Loneliness and having to act on my own may

have made me mature more quickly than most other children. Few under ten are introduced into political circles or are permitted to hear adults' important political decisions.

Indira Gandhi,
PRIME MINISTER OF INDIA

My parents were remarkable, since I was an only child, in always leaving me free to do what I wanted and to be myself. My mother's theory of education was to be quite severe when I was an infant and until I was about ten years old, and then to give me almost absolute freedom of choice.... No one ever said, "Don't climb that tree; you might fall."

May Sarton,
WRITER

When Mom ran away from a home that had completely dominated her, she exploded into a newfound freedom. She drank a lot, loved freely, answered to no one and gave life her best shot. When I was born she had not experienced enough of life—or that newfound freedom—to

This only child landed in Paris in "The Spirit
of St. Louis."

take on the responsibilities of being a mother. I won't say I was an unwanted child, but it was long before "the pill" and, like many young mothers, she was not ready to make the sacrifices required to raise a child. With or without me, Mom still had some living to do. I would be left with a relative or a hired sitter, and if things got good for her, she wouldn't return to pick me up. Often my grandparents or other family members would have to rescue the sitter until Mom showed up. Naturally I don't remember a lot of these things, but you know how it is; even in a family if there is something disagreeable about someone it always gets told. One of Mom's relatives delighted in telling the story of how my mother once sold me for a pitcher of beer. Mom was in a café one afternoon with me in her lap. The waitress, a would-be mother without a child of her own, jokingly told my Mom she'd buy me from her. Mom replied, "A pitcher of beer and he's yours." The waitress set up the beer, Mom stuck around long enough to finish it off and left the place without me. Several days later my uncle had to search the town for the waitress and take me home.

Charles Manson,
MASS MURDERER

This only child married Edward VIII and
became a duchess.

There was one great difference between my father and myself when we were children. He had an elder brother; I had not. So he was never alone in the dark. Lying in bed with the lights out he could so easily "be talking to a dragon" and feeling brave, knowing that if the dragon turned suddenly fierce he had only to reach out a hand and there would be Ken in the next bed. But I could take no such risks.

Christopher Milne,
WRITER AND SON OF A.A. MILNE,
CREATOR OF WINNIE-THE-POOH

A poor peasant sat one evening by his hearth and poked the fire, while his wife sat opposite spinning. He said, "What a sad thing it is that we have no children. Our home is so quiet, while other folk's houses are noisy and cheerful."

"Yes," answered his wife, and she sighed. "Even if it were an only one, and if it were no bigger than my thumb, I should be quite content. We would love it with all our hearts."

Now some time after this she had a little boy who was strong and healthy, but was no bigger than a thumb. Then they said, "Well, our wish is

This only child gave the world
Lord Peter Wimsey.

fulfilled, and small as he is we will love him dearly." And because of his tiny stature they called him Tom Thumb.

(about) Tom Thumb,
FROM THE BROTHERS GRIMM

Other tiny children of fiction and fairy tale who are onlies include Andersen's Thumbelina *and Miss M., in Walter de la Mare's* Memoirs of a Midget.

∞

She was mother, father and big sister to me... and I was son and brother to her, regardless of who she was married to.

Rock Hudson,
ACTOR

∞

My stepmother, who was devotedly attached to me, far too much for my good, was desirous that I should be brought up to live and die "like a gentleman," thinking that fine clothes and filled pockets were the only requisite needed to attain this end. She therefore completely spoiled me, hid my faults, boasted to everyone of my youth-

ful merits, and, worse than all, said frequently in my presence that I was the handsomest boy in France. All my wishes and idle notions were at once gratified; she went so far as actually to grant me *carte blanche* at all the confectionery shops in the town, and also of the village of Coueron, where during the summer we lived, as it were, in the country.

John James Audubon,
NATURALIST AND PAINTER

I'm just an only child—the only child in practically the whole family. It was that phenomenon that made me want to write my first novel— what happened to this family, why are there no kids?

William Kennedy,
NOVELIST

I was so proud of him, even though sometimes he wasn't all that proud of me. You see, as a little girl, I was always being something else; a bird, a lamppost, a policeman, a postman, a flowerpot. I remember the day I decided to be a small dog. I

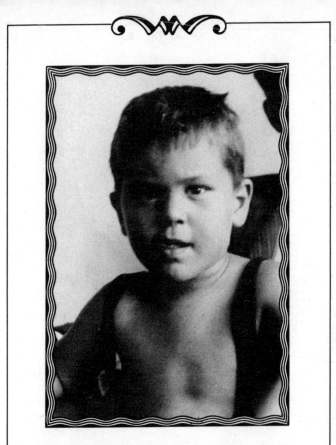

This only child won an Academy Award for his performance as a Mafia don.

was quite disconcerted when my father refused absolutely to put a leash around my neck and take me for a walk. Did him no good though. I still trotted at his heels woofing at all the passers-by and cocking my leg up against every tree we passed. I don't think he was really very happy with the performance, But of course it all came out of being a lonely child.

Ingrid Bergman,
ACTRESS

Bergman's mother died when she was three, her father ten years later. Orphaned at thirteen, she went to live with her aunt, uncle, and five cousins. Nonetheless, "I still went on play-acting in my room."

The reader will have recognized that I was an only child. I was a Caesarian birth, which in those days made it impossible to have more children.... But the reader need waste no sympathy on my solitary state. My toys, my teddy bears and my guinea pigs were all the company I required. I dreaded the efforts that were made to find me companions of my own age. They were always stronger and better fitted for life than I was; they had their own groups of friends and naturally

thought my interests ridiculous. When they left the house I returned with relief to my bears, my bricks, or, at a later date, my billiard table.

Kenneth Clark,
ART HISTORIAN

Lord Clark also proclaimed himself "incapable of any collective activity. I cannot belong to a group. Although I have been elected to nine clubs and have paid the entrance fees, I have resigned from all but one because I have been too embarrassed to speak to any of the members. This is a ridiculous shortcoming, the more so as I am very fond of talking; but I am unable to conquer it."

Perhaps being an only child gives one the ability simply to accept the way things are as they are, without the kind of questions that come with siblings. I came later in my parents' life and simply took the eccentricity of our lives (wandering around Europe to find air clear enough for my father to breathe) for granted. I also wrote my first story when I was five, and my stories and my journal were my companions during an unusually solitary childhood. I am grateful for the oddness

This only child made *Pillow Talk* with Doris Day.

of it, though perhaps in reaction I wanted and had a sizable family of my own.

Madeleine l'Engle
NOVELIST

I had marvelous parents. I was an only child, you see, and had their complete attention. They gave one absolute love.

Iris Murdoch,
NOVELIST

In a separate interview, Murdoch made her feelings about siblings clear: "I wouldn't have tolerated anybody else."

Karen
Eve… why don't you start at the beginning?
Eve
It couldn't possibly interest you.
Margo
Please…
Eve speaks simply and without self-pity:
Eve
I guess it started back home. Wisconsin, that is.

There was just Mum and Dad—and me. I was the only child, and I made believe a lot when I was a kid—I acted out all sorts of things...what they were isn't important. But somehow acting and make-believe began to fill up my life more and more. It got so I couldn't tell the real from the unreal except that the unreal seemed more real to me...I'm talking a lot of gibberish, aren't I?

Lloyd
Not at all...

from *All About Eve,* the 1950 film

Says writer-director Joseph L. Mankiewicz of his creation:
"Watch little girls. Certain little girls, that is. Eve's the one who always seems to wind up at the head of the line for cookies—she'll make or steal her own gold stars to take home if teacher can't be conned into giving her one—she'll throw fits, even run up fake fevers, if the prize is worth it to her. Eve is the one who must inevitably attain Daddy's assurance that he loves her more than he loves Mummy—and goes after the identical assurance from Mummy."

This only child became world-famous in 1958 when he won the Tchaikovsky piano competition in Moscow.

I never associated loneliness with being an only child until my father went to war in 1942. He sent V-mail letters from North Africa, then from England. My mother and I went once a week to the Newsview Theater on Hollywood Boulevard and searched the newsreels for a glimpse of him among the men at war.

George Stevens, Jr.
PRODUCER AND SON OF
DIRECTOR GEORGE STEVENS

The games we played were Nandi games because I knew no others and there was no white child, except myself, anywhere near Njoro, though there may have been some Boer children in the small colony about two hundred miles away on the Uasin Gishu Plateau.

Beryl Markham,
AVIATRIX AND WRITER

Unlike so many only children, Markham always preferred physical activity to any other sort. Hunting and riding in the African bush where she grew up were her early and lasting passions. "Childhood environment," *she later wrote*, "had not inclined me toward a

This only child sang of hound dogs and
heartbreak hotels.

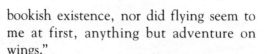

bookish existence, nor did flying seem to me at first, anything but adventure on wings."

∾

There were three of us in that room and a half of ours: my father, my mother and I. A family, a typical Russian family of the time. The time was after the war, and very few people could afford more than one child. Some of them couldn't even afford to have the father alive or present: great terror and war took their toll in big cities, in my hometown especially. So we should have considered ourselves lucky, especially since we were Jews.

Joseph Brodsky,
NOBEL PRIZE–WINNING POET

∾

One of the only places I was ever really, really alone was in the bathroom. I liked it when Nanny went down the hall to Mama's because she'd use the bathroom there and it would give me more time to hole myself up, soaking in the tub. I could have stayed that way for hours, float-

This only child, from an Italian theatrical
family, was one of the most acclaimed actresses
of her day.

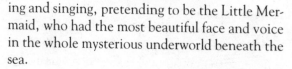

ing and singing, pretending to be the Little Mermaid, who had the most beautiful face and voice in the whole mysterious underworld beneath the sea.

Carol Burnett,
ACTRESS

I spent a good part of my childhood alone. It's not that I was a particularly withdrawn kid, one of those perpetual outsiders. It's just that when I came home from P.S. 197 in Brooklyn, the most pleasurable thing I could think of was to be alone. To daydream. Or to curl up with a book. I'm not sure whether I chose this See-you-later-I'm-closing-my-door route because I was enamored of the worlds in books, or simply because I was desperate to get away from my parents' intensely loving, relentlessly undivided attention.

I never ached with loneliness; the bad news is that as an only child I never learned to share dessert. The good news is that I turned my escapism into a career. I still go into my room and close my door. What do you do for a living, Ms. Isaacs? Well, I hang out by myself and daydream.

Susan Isaacs,
NOVELIST

A bewildered vermin and stray, without reason or purpose, I escaped into the family play-acting, twisting and turning, running, flying from imposture to imposture. I fled from my unjustifiable body and its dreary confidences. If the spinning top collided with an obstacle and stopped, the frenzied little ham would relapse into an animal stupor. Good friends said to my mother that I was sad, that they had seen me dreaming. My mother hugged me to her, with a laugh: "You who are so gay, always singing! What could you possibly complain about? You have everything you want." She was right. A spoiled child isn't sad; he's bored, like a king. Like a dog.

Jean-Paul Sartre,
PHILOSOPHER

∽

Yes, I think as a child I did better with my back to the wall—in extreme situations, among strangers. Whatever strangers could do to me, they could not bite, and there was the hope I might never meet them again. It was my near ones, my dear ones, the fond, the anxious, the proud-of-me, who set up the inhibition. I could not endure their hopes; I could not bear to fail under loving eyes. I detested causing a disappointment.

This only child was *Indiscreet* with Ingrid
Bergman, another only, and portrayed Cole
Porter—yet another—on screen.

Perhaps I exaggerated the disappointment? Perhaps I did less badly than I imagined? You see, it mattered too much. I shall never know.

Elizabeth Bowen,
WRITER

If only, I think, playing with my sunrise shell—if only we could have each of our children alone, not just for part of each day, but for part of each month, each year. Would they not be happier, stronger, and, in the end, more independent because more secure? Does each child not secretly long for the relationship he once had with the mother, when he was "The Baby," when the nursery doors were shut and she was feeding him at her breast—*alone*? And if we were able to put into practice this belief and spend more time with each child alone—would he not only gain in security and strength, but also learn an important first lesson in his adult relationship?

Anne Morrow Lindbergh,
WRITER

This advice comes from the mother of five—herself not an only child.

This only child, a Swedish actress, starred
in such disparate films as *Casablanca* and
Cactus Flower.

Here are some other only children:

William A. Anders
Emmanuel Ax
Burt Bacharach
Pierre Balmain
James Beard
Romare Bearden
Ann Beattie
Isaiah Berlin
Elizabeth Bishop
Eubie Blake
Lisa Bonet
Frank Borman
Ed Bradley
Bill Bradley
Heywood Hale Broun
Blair Brown
Truman Capote
Dick Cavett
Claude Chabrol
Raymond Chandler
Carol Channing
Jacques Chirac
Eric Clapton
Eldridge Cleaver

Roy Cohn
Joseph Conrad
Tom Conti
Elvis Costello
Richard Daley
Leonardo da Vinci
Pam Dawber
C. Day-Lewis
Christopher Durang
Linda Ellerbee
Perry Ellis
Robert Englund
Paul Erdös
Vladimir Feltsman
Fred W. Friendly
Clark Gable
William Gaddis
Frank Gilroy
Nadine Gordimer
Louis Gossett, Jr.
Arthur Hailey
Radclyffe Hall
Mark Hatfield
Tom Hayden

This only child created unforgettable photographs
of the High Sierras and Yosemite Valley.

William Randolph
  Hearst
Charlton Heston
Patricia Highsmith
Eric Hoffer
John Houseman
Barbara Hutton
Carl C. Icahn
Eric Idle
Elton John
James Earl Jones
Shirley Jones
Gary Kasparov
Neil Kinnock
Dean Koontz
C. Everett Koop
Ted Koppel
Jerzy Kosinski
Swoosie Kurtz
Marquis de Lafayette
Hedy Lamarr
Peter Lawford
Ivan Lendl
Annie Lennox
Shelley Long
H.P. Lovecraft
James A. Lovell
Robert Lowell

Daniel K. Ludwig
Ross Macdonald
Anna Magnani
Maria Goeppert Mayer
Peter Max
Ann Miller
Grace Mirabella
Joe Montana
Maria Montessori
Farley Mowat
Anthony Newley
Jack Nicholson
Flannery O'Connor
Al Pacino
Alan Parker
Robert Edwin Peary
George Peppard
S.J. Perelman
Anthony Perkins
T. Boone Pickens
Harold Pinter
Elvis Presley
Harold Prince
Rex Reed
Frederick Remington
Pete Rozelle
Margaret Rutherford
Robert Ryan

Jill St. John
Antonin Scalia
George Schultz
Peter Sellers
Aleksandr
  Solzhenitsyn
Mickey Spillane
Susan Stamberg
Ringo Starr
Roger Staubach
William Styron
Jacqueline Susann
Renata Tebaldi
Michael Tilson
  Thomas

Jean Toomer
François Truffaut
Sarah Vaughan
Violette Verdy
Nicholas von Hoffman
Alan Watts
Betty White
Edward Bennett
  Williams
Edmund Wilson
Gahan Wilson
John Wood
Tammy Wynette
Marguerite Yourcenar

SOURCES

Hans Christian Andersen, *The Story of My Life* (Hurd & Houghton, 1872).

Eve Arden, *The Three Phases of Eve* (St. Martin's, 1985).

Brooke Astor, *Footprints* (Doubleday, 1980).

Mary Astor, *My Story* (Doubleday, 1959).

John James Audubon, *Journals,* vol. 2, edited by Marie R. Audubon (Scribner's, 1897).

A. J. Ayer, *Part of My Life* (Harcourt Brace Jovanovich, 1977).

Ingrid Bergman and Alan Burgess, *My Story* (Delacorte, 1980).

Elizabeth Bowen, *The Mulberry Tree: Writings of Elizabeth Bowen,* edited by Hermione Lee (Harcourt Brace Jovanovich, 1986).

Jane Bowles, described in *A Little Original Sin,* by Millicent Dillon (Holt, Rinehart & Winston, 1981).

Paul Bowles, *Without Stopping* (Putnam's, 1972).

Joseph Brodsky, *Less Than One: Selected Essays* (Farrar Straus Giroux, 1986).

Carol Burnett, *One More Time: A Memoir* (Random House, 1987).

Jackie Chan, interviewed by Hilda C. Wang (*The New York Times*, August 16, 1987).

Kenneth Clark, *Another Part of the Wood: A Self-Portrait* (Harper & Row, 1974).

Cyril Connolly, *Enemies of Promise* (Little, Brown 1939).

Divine, interviewed by Stephanie Mansfield (*The Washington Post,* February 26, 1988).

Eleonora Duse, letter quoted in *Eleonora Duse: A Biography,* by William Weaver (Harcourt Brace Jovanovich, 1984).

Loren Eiseley, *All the Strange Hours: The Excavation of a Life* (Scribner's, 1975).

Indira Gandhi, *Letters to an American Friend: 1950–1984,* edited, with commentary, from correspondence with Dorothy Norman (Harcourt Brace Jovanovich, 1986).

Romain Gary, *Promise at Dawn* (Harper & Row, 1961).

Mikhail Gorbachev, referred to in *Time* (January 4, 1988).

Glenn Gould, quoted in "The Apollonian," by Joseph Roddy (*The New Yorker,* 1960).

Alec Guinness, *Blessings in Disguise* (Knopf, 1986).

Lillian Hellman, *An Unfinished Woman* (Little, Brown, 1969).

Rock Hudson and Sara Davidson, *Rock Hudson: My Story* (Morrow, 1986).

William Kennedy, interviewed by Curt Suplee
(*The Washington Post,* December 28, 1983).

R.D. Laing, *Wisdom, Madness and Folly: The Making of a Psychiatrist* (McGraw-Hill, 1985).

Anne Morrow Lindbergh, *Gift from the Sea* (Pantheon, 1955).

Charles Manson, *Manson in His Own Words,* as told to Nuel Emmons (Grove, 1986).

Beryl Markham, *West with the Night* (North Point Press, 1983).

Christopher Milne, *The Enchanted Places* (Dutton, 1975).

John Mortimer, *Clinging to the Wreckage* (Ticknor & Fields, 1982).

Iris Murdoch, interviewed by James Atlas (*Vanity Fair,* March, 1988); also, interviewed by Ned Geeslin and Fred Hauptfuhrer (*People,* March 14, 1988).

Frank O'Connor, *An Only Child* (Knopf, 1961).

Anna Pavlova, quoted in *Pavlova: Portrait of a Dancer,* presented by Margot Fonteyn (Viking, 1984).

David Rieff, *Going To Miami* (Little, Brown, 1987).

Rainer Maria Rilke, quoted in *A Ringing Glass: The Life of Rainer Maria Rilke*, by Donald Prater (Oxford University Press, 1986).

Vita Sackville-West, quoted in *Portrait of a Marriage,* by Nigel Nicolson (Atheneum, 1972).

May Sarton, *A World of Light* (Norton, 1976).

Jean-Paul Sartre, *The Words,* translated by Bernard Frechtman (Braziller, 1964).

Simone Signoret, *Nostalgia Isn't What It Used To Be,* translated by Cornelia Schaeffer (Harper & Row, 1978).

Frank Sinatra, quoted in *Frank Sinatra: My Father,* by Nancy Sinatra (Doubleday, 1985).

Frank Sinatra, described in *His Way: The Unauthorized Biography of Frank Sinatra,* by Kitty Kelley (Bantam, 1986).

Harry Stack Sullivan, *The Interpersonal Theory of Psychiatry,* edited by Helen Swick Perry and Mary Ladd Gawel (Norton, 1953).

Gloria Swanson, *Swanson on Swanson* (Random House, 1980).

Margaret Truman, *Letters from Father* (Arbor House, 1981).

John Updike, from *Five Boyhoods,* edited by Martin Levin (Doubleday, 1962).

Jonathan Winters, interviewed by Cleveland Amory *(Parade Magazine,* December 20, 1987).

Norma E. Cutts and Nicholas Moseley, *The Only Child: A Guide for Parents and Children of All Ages* (Putnam's, 1954).

E. A. Davis, "The Development of Linguistic Skill in Twins, etc." (University of Minnesota Press, Institute of Child Welfare Series, No. 14, 1937).

Sidonie Matsner Gruenberg, "Changing Conceptions of the Family" (*Annals of the American Academy of Political and Social Science*, May, 1947).

G. Stanley Hall, "The Contents of Children's Minds" (*Princeton Review*, 1883).

Lena H. Sun, "The Spoiled Brats of China" (*The Washington Post*, July 26, 1987).

Anthony Burgess, *A Clockwork Orange* (W.W. Norton, 1962).

Jacob and Wilhelm Grimm, *Fairy Tales*, in translations by Lucy Crane, Marian Edwardes, Mrs. Edgar Lucas, and Others (World, 1947).

Joseph L. Mankiewicz, *All About Eve: A Screenplay*. Based upon a short story by Mary Orr (Random House, 1951).

Joseph L. Mankiewicz and Gary Carey, *More About All About Eve: A Colloquy* (Random House, 1972).

George D. Painter, *Marcel Proust*, Vol. 1 (Random House, 1959).

Marcel Proust, *Swann's Way 1923, Remembrance of Things Past,* translated by C.K. Scott Moncrieff and Terence Kilmartin (Random House, 1981).

KEY TO PHOTOGRAPHS

HELP!

For parents who want to raise their children better... and for the adults those children will become.